Thomas Bennet

God in Christ

A wall of fire round about the church, and the glory in the midst of her:

being a sermon, preached at Milnathort before the associate presbytery

of Kirkcaldie: January 8. 1774

Thomas Bennet

God in Christ
A wall of fire round about the church, and the glory in the midst of her: being a sermon, preached at Milnathort before the associate presbytery of Kirkcaldie: January 8. 1774

ISBN/EAN: 9783337042318

Printed in Europe, USA, Canada, Australia, Japan

Cover: Foto ©Lupo / pixelio.de

More available books at **www.hansebooks.com**

THOMAS BENNET

Minister of the Gospel to the Associate Congregation

ZEPH. iii. 16, 17.

*In that day it shall be said to Jerusalem, Fear thou not: And to Zion
thine hands be slack. The Lord thy God in the midst of thee
he will save, he will rejoice over thee with joy: He will r
love, he will joy over thee with singing.*

EDINBURGH:

PRINTED in the Year 1777.

ZECH. ii. 5.

For I, faith the Lord, will be unto her a wall of fire round about, and will be the glory in the midft of her.

THE Prophet Zechariah, prophefied at the fame time with Haggai. They both began their public miniſtrations much about eighteen years after the return of the Church from her captivity in Babylon ; when the building of Jerufalem and the Temple, was both greatly retarded by its enemies, and neglected by its friends.

The main fcope of the Prophet, in this prophecy, is to excite and forward the Jews to the building up of Jerufalem ; and, being encouraged by gracious viſions and revelations, refpecting the fuccefs and profperity of the work : He animated the hearts, and ftrengthened the hands of the builders, by laying before them the fame grounds of confolation, whereby he was comforted : And, under the good hand of God, the work was carried forward, and that, over the belly of all oppofition made thereto, from whatever quarter it did arife.

In the preceding chapter, the Prophet has two fpecial and comforting viſions : The one, of a man among the myrtle-trees, which were in the bottom, that is, of Chriſt in his defpifed Church. The other, of four horns, (by which we are to underftand the enemies of the Church); and of as many carpenters, by whom thefe horns were to be cut off.

In this chapter, he has another pleafant difcovery. He fees a man with a meafuring line in his hand, whereby he is given to know, that Jerufalem fhould be built ; and the Temple reared up. And, as the oppofition made to the work was to be managed both with open violence, and a load of the moft contemptuous reproach. In the words of the text, the Lord engages himfelf by promife, to defend them from both thefe kinds of perfecution : From open violence, by being a wall of fire

about

about Jerufalem ; and from reproach, by being the glory in the midft of her. For " I, faith the Lord, will be " unto her a wall of fire round about, and will be the " glory in the midft of her." Glorious things indeed, are here fpoken of the city of our God : And were faith in exercife, with what pleafure and delight, would we both fpeak and hear of them ? This promife, is a moft enriching, and comforting legacy left to the Church ; the believing improvement of which, will not fail to afford her the fweeteft confolation in the very worft of times.

In the words we may obferve, 1. The Author of the promife pointed out in the pronoun *I*. *I*, faith the Lord ; *I*, who am Jerufalem's God in covenant, her Saviour and Redeemer ; the Mighty One of Jacob her King. *I*, who am both able and ready, to do all for her, which her condition at any time, can poffibly call for at my hand.

2. We may obferve the object of the promife, *Jerufalem*, that is the Church of God, the fpiritual Jerufalem, called Mount Zion, and the city of the living God, Heb. xii. 22. For, though the promife fpeaks primarily and immediately concerning the fafety and glory of the earthly Jerufalem, in which did dwell the worldly fanctuary : It is intended, ultimately and chiefly, to fet furth the fafety and glory of the heavenly Jerufalem, or the gofpel Church ; as is abundantly obvious from the fcope and defign of this whole prophefy.

3. We may obferve the promife itfelf, confifting of two branches.

The *firft* fetting forth, that prefervation which the Lord vouchfafes to his Church and people, from that kind of perfecution which is often carried on againft them with open violence and rage. " I, faith the Lord, will be unto " her a wall of fire round about Jerufalem :" As if the Lord had faid, tho' at prefent in a very defencelefs ftate, and as yet without a material wall ; fhe need not be afraid, for I will be unto her a wall, and that of the moft impregnable nature ; a wall of fire. A wall in which there fhall not be the fmalleft breach. It fhall be round about her : So that from whatfoever quarter the enemy may attempt to affault her, he fhall not prevail againft her.

In

In this branch of the promife, there may be an allufion to the cuftom of travellers in the eaftern countries, who, when they pitched their tents, kindled fires round about them, to deter lions, or other wild beafts, from falling upon them, or difturbing their repofe. Or to that aftonifhingly glorious fymbol of the divine prefence, the pillar of cloud and fire, which accompanied Ifrael from Egypt into the promifed land : And by which, they were not only led and directed in their feveral journies, but alfo protected from the fury of their raging adverfaries. To this the Prophet Ifaiah evidently refers, in a promife moft fimilar to this, chap. iv. 5. " And the Lord will " create upon every dwelling-place of mount Zion, and " upon her affemblies, a cloud and fmoke by day, and " the fhining of a flaming fire by night : For upon all " the glory fhall be a defence."

The *fecond* branch of the promife, prefents us with the Church's defence from the fcourge of the tongue ; " And will be the glory in the midft of her." God has taken up his reft in fpiritual Jerufalem, he is known in her palaces for a refuge ; and from thence, he fhines forth as her glory. He is often faid to be in the midft of the Church, Ifa. xii. 6. and to walk in the midft of the Church, Rev. i. 13. And when he faith, *I will be the glory in the midft of her*, refpect may be had to the pofition of the Ark in the congregation of Ifrael, while they journeyed unto the typical reft. It was fituate in the midft of the congregation ; and being eminently typical of our Lord Jefus Chrift, is therefore called the glory of Ifrael, 1 Sam. iv. 21.

4. *Laftly*, We may obferve the certainty of the promife, as to its accomplifhment. " I, faith the Lord, will " be unto her a wall of fire round about, and will be the " glory in the midft of her." The Lord hath faid it, and therefore, let Jerufalem believe it for her comfort ; and her enemies to their confufion. God hath fpoken in his holinefs, let us take pleafure in it ; and firmly truft his faithful word : For he is not a man, that he fhould lie: Nor the fon of man, that he fhould repent.

DOCT.

Doct. It is fufficient matter and ground of comfort to the Church in the very worft of times, that a God in Chrift, has engaged himfelf by promife, to be a wall of fire round about her, and the glory in the midft of her. " I, faith the Lord, will be unto her a wall of fire round " about, and will be the glory in the midft of her."

The doctrine being evident from the text, in difcourfing from it, through grace, I fhall endeavour to obferve the following method.

I. I would mention fome things implied in the promife contained in the text.

II. Speak of the Lord as a wall of fire round about his Church and people.

III. Enquire in what refpects he may be faid to be the glory in the midft of the Church.

IV. Offer fome reafons, why the Lord has engaged himfelf by promife, to be a wall of fire round about the Church, and the glory in the midft of her.

V. Apply.

The firft thing, is to mention fome things implied in the promife. And,

1ft, The promife implies that the Church hath many enemies. That fhe needs a wall, a wall round about her ; and fuch a wall as the text informs us of, plainly demon-ftrates, that fhe has her enemies round about her alfo. The Church is often fet upon by perfecution and open violence ; fhe is frequently infefted with hereticks and falfe teachers, 2 Pet. ii. 1. " But there were falfe prophets " alfo among the people, even as there fhall be falfe " teachers among you, who fhall bring in privily damnable " herefies, even denying the Lord who bought them, and " bring upon themfelves fwift deftruction." Zion is oft in danger, even from the fons fhe has brought up. Hence, the Apoftle Paul tells the elders of the Church of Ephe-fus, that even of their ownfelves, men fhould arife fpeak-ing perverfe things, to draw away difciples after them, Acts xx. 30. And as we have heard from the Holy Ghoft, fpeaking in his word ; fo have we feen it, in the city of

our

our God. There have been from the beginning, and to the
end there will be, fome to oppofe the purity of gofpel
doctrine in the Church ; fome to oppofe her government
and difcipline, and others to endeavour to caft the veil of
fuperftition and will-worfhip over the purity and fimplicity
of her divinely inftituted acts of worfhip and homage.
The Church and people of God, are an eye-fore to Satan
and a prophane world ; and therefore they are continually
plotting mifchief againft them. Hence is that exhortation,
1 Pet. v. 8. " Be fober, be vigilant, for your ·adverfary
" the devil, as a roring lion, walketh about feeking whom
" he may devour." Our Lord warns his difciples, and
in them all his followers, to the end, that what they have
to expect from the world, is tribulation, John xiii. 33.
In the world ye fhall have tribulation.

2. The promife implies, that the Church in herfelf confidered, is no equal match for her enemies. She, comparatively confidered, is but a fmall city, and her inhabitants
few and weak. The Church is but a little flock. The
fheep of Chrift's pafture are but as a few lambs in the
midft of many ravening wolves. The Church and people
of God have found caufe, in all ages, to adopt the language
of Jehofhaphat, 2 Chron. xx. 12. " We have no might
" againft this great company that cometh againft us ;"
and, to join with the Pfalmift, fpeaking in the name of the
Church, Pfal. cxxiv. 2, 3, 4. " If it had not been the
" Lord who was on our fide, when men rofe up againft
" us ; then they had fwallowed us up quick, when their
" wrath was kindled againft us : Then the waters had
" overwhelmed us, the ftream had gone over our foul."

3. The promife implies, that however weak the Church
is, in herfelf confidered, fhe has a fufficiency of ftrength
in her glorious Head, to overmatch the power and policy
of her moft potent and fubtile adverfaries, " I, faith the
" Lord, will be unto her a wall of fire round about, and
" will be the glory in the midft of her." The Lord of
Hofts is ever upon her fide, and the God of Jacob is her
refuge, Pfal. xlvi. 7. However many and ftrong her enemies be, her King paffes on before her, and Jehovah is on
her head ; and all her enemies muft be found liars,

Micah

Micah ii. 13. " The breaker is come up before them:
" They have broken up, and have paffed through the
" gate, and are gone out by it; their King fhall pafs be-
" fore them, and the Lord on the head of them," Deut.
xxxiii. 29. " Happy art thou, O Ifrael: who is like unto
" thee, O people faved by the Lord; the fhield of thy
" help, and who is the fword of thy excellency! and thine
" enemies fhall be found liars unto thee, and thou fhalt
" tread upon their high places."

4. The promife implies admirable condefcenfion in God,
he condefcends to our fimilitudes, and fo to adapt himfelf
to our weak capacities, as to fet himfelf in every light
that may tend moft for the comfort of his people in the
day of trial. Are they at any time expofed to open violence? Then, he tells them, *He will be a wall of fire
round about them.* Are they at any time expofed to reproach? And, (tho' the excellent ones of the earth)
counted as the off-fcouring of all things? Then, he af-
fures them, *he will be the glory in the midft of them.*
However low therefore, they may at any time be brought
by their enemies; they have always caufe to triumph in
him, faying with the Prophet in name of the Church,
" Rejoice not againft me, O mine enemies: When I fall,
" I fhall arife; when I fit in darknefs, the Lord fhall be
" a light unto me. I will bear the indignation of the
" Lord, becaufe I have finned againft him, until he plead
" my caufe, and execute judgment for me: He will bring
" me forth to the light, and I fhall behold his righteouf-
" nefs. Then fhe that is mine enemy fhall fee it, and
" fhame fhall cover her who faid unto me, Where is the
" Lord thy God? Mine eyes fhall behold her: Now
" fhall fhe be troden down as the mire of the ftreets."

5. The promife implies, that the fafety, beauty, and
glory of the Church ftand and fall together. In the cafe
of any particular Church, the Lord is no longer a wall of
fire round about her, than he is the glory in the midft
of her. When any Church lets go her glory; the glory
of purity in her doctrine; the glory of a faithful and impartial exercife of the fword of difcipline; the glorious
order and government her Head has appointed in her;
                                                    with

with the purity and fpirituality of her worfhip: However happy fhe may look on herfelf to be, from fome external confiderations, fuch as the favour and protection of
the potentates of the earth ; yet her defence is in reality
departed from her.   We fee in the cafe of God's profef-
fing people of old, when once the glory of the God of
Ifrael was gone up from the Cherub, whereupon it was,
to the threfhold of the houfe ; they foon found themfelves
deprived of their fafe-guard and defence, Ezek. ix. 1,—5.
How far the glory in the above refpects, is departed from
the Churches of Britain and Ireland, and in a particular
manner from the Church of Scotland, is no lefs vifible
than lamentable, to every fpiritual obferver.   And it is no
lefs to be lamented, that zeal for the declarative glory of
God, and a concern for the maintenance of purity, in doctrine, difcipline, worfhip, and government, is greatly upon
the decline, even among thofe who have been led out to
efpoufe a teftimony for the fame.   Iniquity is abounding,
and, alas ! our love is waxing cold.   We may, with too
much propriety, adopt the Apoftle's complaint, Phil. ii. 21.
" All feek their own, not the things which are Jefus
" Chrift's."

6. The promife implies, that as the Church and people
of God, have in reality nothing to fear in the way of their
walking with God, and worthy of him : So, he would
not have them to give way to defpondency ; whatever
oppofition they may meet with from hell and earth in
the way of duty.   There were many to oppofe the
building of Jerufalem, and the inftruments to be employ-
ed in the work, but comparatively few in number, and
their ftrength fmall : Yet, the Lord would have them
take courage, and not be afraid ; feeing, he would be a
wall of fire round about them, and the glory in the midft
of them.   And to the fame purpofe is that promife, Ifa.
xliii. 2. " When thou paffeft through the waters, I will be
" with thee ; and through the rivers, they fhall not over-
" flow thee : When thou walkeft through the fire, thou
" fhalt not be burnt ; neither fhall the flame kindle upon
" thee."

B   7. Laftly,

7. *Lastly*, The promise implies, that the believing consideration of what the Lord has from the beginning done for the Church, and what he has promised he will continue to do to, and for her, unto the end, is more than sufficient to support her under the sorest pressures and calamities, she may at any time be trusted with. When the Church in general, or the particular believer begins to give way to desponding fears, it is not on account of the number and strength of the enemy, but the want of faith in a promising God. It was not the number and strength of the inhabitants of Canaan, that made the men Moses sent to spy the land, despair of getting the victory over them; Num. xiii. 25. But their want of faith in the promise; Psal. cv. 11. " Unto thee will I give the " land of Canaan, the lot of your inheritance."

II. The *second* head in the method, was to speak of the Lord as a wall of fire about his Church and people. Where,

First, We may take a view of the wall itself. *Secondly*, Of the nature and quality of it, as set forth in the text, *a wall of fire*.

Then, as to the wall, It is God himself. " I, saith the " Lord, will be unto her a wall of fire round about." As " the mountains are round about Jerusalem, so the " Lord is round about his people, from henceforth," Psal. cxxv. 2. All the perfections and attributes of the divine nature, as displayed and manifested in the person of our Lord Jesus Christ, harmoniously conspire in making up this wall. His omnipresence, his omniscience, wisdom, power, immutability, mercy, love, and faithfulness. And to these, we may add, the hedge of his special providence, which, Satan, the head of all that opposition which is at any time made against the Church, found to be a wall of fire, through which, he was by no means able to penetrate; hence saith he, " Hast thou not made a hedge about him, " (to wit, Job,) and about his house, and about all that " he hath on every side? Thou hast blessed the work of " his hands, and his substance is increased."

2*d*, As to the nature of this wall, we are told, that it is of fire. And we think, the expression is intended.

1st, To

1*ſt*, To ſet furth the terrible Majeſty, in which the Lord is ſometimes pleaſed to appear in behalf of his Church and People, and againſt their enemies. A wall of fire muſt be very terrible ; and with God is terrible majeſty. Accordingly, we find, that when he was executing his awful, though juſt judgments upon the Canaanites, he is ſaid to have gone before his People as flaming fire ; Deut. ix. 3. " Underſtand therefore, this day," ſaith Moſes to Iſrael, " that the Lord thy God is he that goeth over be-" fore thee, as a confuming fire." The Lord is ſometimes pleaſed to anſwer the prayers of his oppreſſed heritage, in the way of inflicting moſt affecting judgments upon their enemies, Pſal. lxv. 5. 2 Chron. xxxii. 20, 21. And the tremenduous appearance our Lord Jeſus is to make to all his enemies at the laſt day, we are told, is to be in flaming fire ; 2 Theſ. i. 7. 8. " The Lord Jeſus ſhall be " revealed from heaven with his mighty angels, in flam-" ing fire, taking vengeance on them that know not God, " and obey not the goſpel of our Lord Jeſus Chriſt."

2. The manner of expreſſion intimates, that the pro-tection the Lord vouchſafes to grant to his Church and people, is ſometimes no leſs manifeſt and viſible, than ter-rible and affecting to their enemies. Many viſible proofs and evidences, has the Lord condeſcended to give of his regard for his Church, and of his diſpleaſure with his and her enemies. So obſervable were his judgments upon Egypt, that even the miniſters of Satan, behoved to ac-knowledge, that the finger of God was in them ; Exod. viii. 19. " Then the magicians ſaid unto Pharaoh, This " is the finger of God." And ſo manifeſt was the Lord's hand in the deliverance of the Church from her thraldom and bondage in Babylon, That ſhe did not only ſee it her-ſelf, but even the heathen were obliged to acknowledge his might, Pſal. cxxvi. 2. " Then ſaid they among the " heathen, The LORD hath done great things for them." Moſt ſignal have the appearances been which the Lord has been pleaſed to make in behalf of his Church in theſe lands ; particularly, at our Reformation from pope-ry, and at the memorable Revolution, when he cut the cords of an ungodly crew, when uſing all their power

and

and policy to wreath the yoke of Popery again about our necks. And we have reafon to acknowledge to his praife, that, fince that time, he has been pleafed, once and again to blaft the defigns of the emiffaries of the man of fin, when intending to deprive us of our moft precious liberties, both civil and religious.

3. The expreffion intimates, that God is an active defence to his people. A wall of fire, muft not only defend and bear off an enemy; but it muft exceedingly offend and diftrefs thofe againft whom it flames. Though God is often pleafed, for wife and holy ends and purpofes, to bear long with his, and his peoples enemies; yet, when his patience and long-fuffering is abufed by them, inftead of their being thereby led to repentance, he will whet his glittering fword, and his hand will take hold of judgment, and then fhall he render a recompence to his enemies; yea, " the Lord fhall fwallow them up in his wrath, and " the fire fhall devour them, Pfal. xxi. 9." Sentence not being always fpeedily executed againft an evil work, the worker is ready to conclude, That God is like himfelf, and that he approves of his fin, Pfal. l. 21. But let poor deluded adverfaries to God, and his Church and people, confider, that if they finally perfift in their enmity to the Lord, and his hidden ones; their violent dealing will inevitably fall upon their own guilty heads; Pfal. lxviii. 21. " God fhall wound the head of his enemies; and the hairy " fcalp of fuch a one as goeth on ftill in his trefpaffes."

4. When the Lord faith, he will be unto the Church a wall of fire round about; as much is intimated, as that he is an impregnable defence unto her. There is no breaking in upon a wall of fire. It is true indeed, the Lord is fometimes pleafed, for wife and holy purpofes, to fuffer his Church in general, and the believer in particular, to be brought very low by their enemies, before he interpofe for their deliverance. This has moft frequently been the cafe, and will continue to be the cafe with the Church while in her militant ftate: But fuch difpenfations of providence, have been, and ftill fhall be fo over-ruled and managed by infinite wifdom, love, and grace, as that they tend in the event to promote and advance her real good

and

and fpiritual welfare : For he abideth faithful, who hath faid, "Upon this rock I will build my Church ; and the "gates of hell fhall not prevail againft her," Matth. xvi. 18. And, fays the Apoftle, Rom. viii. 28. "We know that "all things work together for good to them who love "God, to them who are the called according to his pur- "pofe."

5. *Laftly*, The manner of expreffion intimates, that all who fight againft mount Zion, they rufh upon devouring fire. All the enemies of God and his Church, are but as briers and thorns before the fiery flame ; through which her God can moft eafily break, and burn them up together ; Ifa. xxvii. 4. "Who would fet the briers and thorns "againft me in battle ? I would go through them, I "would burn them *up* together." And of God's faithful witneffes, we are told, that fire proceedeth out of their mouth, whereby their enemies are devoured ; Rev. xi. 5. "And if any man will hurt them, fire proceedeth out of "their mouth, and devoureth their adverfaries : And if "any man will hurt them, he muft in this manner be "killed."

III. The *third* head in the method, was to enquire in what refpects the Lord may be faid to be the glory in the midft of the Church. And,

1. It has been the privilege of the Church, to have her God in the midft of her, in refpect of his prefence with her in human nature. Her God in the perfon of the Son, was pleafed to become a partaker of flefh and blood ; and for a feafon, was pleafed to fojourn with her upon the earth ; John i. 14. "The Word was made flefh, and "dwelt among us (and we beheld his glory, the glory as "of the only begotten of the Father) full of grace and "truth." In this refpect he called himfelf the light and glory of the world, in a moft fingular manner ; John ix. 5. "As long as I am in the world, I am the light of the "world." But, as it was not expedient he fhould con- tinue with the Church on earth, in refpect of bodily pre- fence, after he had glorified God here, and finifhed the work given him to do : His prefence with the Church in
this

this respect, is no more to be expected : The heavens having long since received him, and that until the restitution of all things.

2. He is the glory in the midst of the Church, in respect of his real gracious and spiritual presence. Hence saith he to his disciples, a little before his departure from them, as to his bodily presence ; " Yet a little while, and " the world seeth me no more ; but ye see me : Because " I live, ye shall live also," John. xiv. 19. At his ascension, the last words, it is probable, which the disciples heard him express, contained that most gracious and comforting promise, we have ; Math. xxviii. 19, 20. That he would be present with his Church, in and by his spirit, until the mystery of God shall be finished. And after his reception into glory, the beloved disciple had, in vision, a most comfortable view of him as in the midst of the Church, Rev. i. 13. And I saw, " In the midst of the se- " ven candlesticks, one like unto the Son of man, clothed " with a garment down to the foot, and girt about the " paps with a golden girdle." Yea, the very name of the gospel Jerusalem, is, The LORD is there ; Ezek. xlviii. 35. " It was round about eighteen thousand measures : " And the name of the city from that day shall be, THE " LORD IS THERE."

3. He is the glory in the midst of the Church in respect of his ordinances, which are the symbols of his presence. There is a real beauty and glory in divine ordinances ; and that, both in themselves considered, and in the eye of all spiritual discerners ; however mean and contemptible they may appear in the sight of a carnal world. They are all marked with the beautifying stamp of his authority, and in and by them, he is pleased to manifest the glory of his power, love, grace, and wisdom. His people see his power and glory in his holy place ; Psal. lxiii. 2. The ordinances of God, have in them more glory and beauty to the believing soul, than tongue can fully express. Hence they are disposed to cry out with wonder, " How amiable " are thy tabernacles, O Lord of hosts !" Psal. lxxxiv. 1. And with what esteem and regard, do we find the spouse speaking of divine ordinances ? Cant. i. 16. " Our bed is " green

" green, (fays fhe) the beams of our houfe are cedar,
" and our rafters of fir."

4. He is the glory in the midft of the Church in refpect
of faithful gofpel Minifters, who are his gift to the
Church; Eph. iv. 11, 12. Faithful minifters, are the ambaffadors of the Prince of Peace ; Eph. iv. 20. Hence
faith the Apoftle, 2 Cor. v. 20. " Now we are ambaffadors
" for Chrift, as though God did befeech you by us ; we
" pray you in Chrift's ftead, be ye reconciled unto God."
And as they are the ambaffadors of Chrift, he may be faid
in refpect of them, to be reprefentatively prefent with the
Church, in and by their miniftry. Hence they are called
the glory of Chrift, 2 Cor. viii. 13. And they are fo,
only in fo far as he is pleafed to manifeft his glory in and
by them, unto the Church.

5. *Laftly,* He is the glory in the midft of the Church,
in regard, that all the beauty and glory of the Church, is
from him, and all centers in him. All that glorious grace
any of the fons of men are made partakers of, is from
him. True Church-members, are glorious within ; and
their cloathing is of wrought gold, Pfal. xlv. 13. But all
this beauty and glory, in which the faints do fhine in the
kingdom of grace here, and fhall fhine as the brightnefs of
the firmament in the kingdom of glory, is only through
his comelinefs put upon them : And the glory of all they
are, and of all that, by his grace, they are made to enjoy, will forever center in him, in their harmonioufly
united expreffions of eternal praife and thankfgiving in
the Jerufalem above: According to the Apoftle's earneft
wifh, Eph. iii. 21. " Unto him be glory in the Church
" by Chrift Jefus, throughout all ages, world without
" end. Amen."

IV. The *fourth* head in the method, was to enquire,
wherefore the Lord has engaged himfelf by promife, to
be a wall of fire about the church, and the glory in the
midft of her? And 1ft, This muft be refolved in fovereignty. All the promifes, and this among the reft, take their
rife from free, rich, and fovereign love and grace ; and
not from any good qualifications, real or fuppofed, in the
objects they refpect: Hence the promifes are faid to be
given

given us in a teſtamentary way; 2 Pet. i. 4. And the Lord gives the prophet Ezekel commandment, to ſay unto the houſe of Iſrael, " Thus ſaith the Lord God, I do " not this for your ſakes, O houſe of Iſrael, but for mine " holy name's ſake." Chap. xxxvi. 22.

2. He has done ſo, becauſe of his great love to the Church : He loved her from everlaſting; Jer. xxxi. 3. When the fulneſs of the time was come, he gave himſelf for her, in the perſon of his Son ; Eph. v. 2. 1 John iii. 16. He purchaſed her with his own blood; Acts, xx. 28. And ſuch is his love to her, that ſhe is as a ſeal upon his very heart; Cant. viii. 6. And her walls are continually before him; Iſa. xlix. 16. Yea, ſo dear are his people unto him, that whoſoever toucheth them to their hurt ; they touch the apple of his eye ; Zech. ii. 8. " He that " toucheth you, toucheth the apple of his eye."

3. He has promiſed to be a wall of fire about the Church, and the glory in the midſt of her, becauſe of her natural weakneſs. The Church is weak in herſelf conſidered, and ſhe has many enemies to contend with. Many and great are the trials which the Lord in holy providence, ſees meet to permit his Church and people to fall under ; and for their encouragement amidſt them all, and leſt they ſhould ſink and faint under them, he has given them moſt gracious aſſurances, that he will not fail to be their help in the day of trouble : But will moſt effectually ſuccour and ſupport them againſt every aſſault of their adverſaries, whether from without, or from within. The Church may now know in her experience, " That her " enemies have often come in upon her like a flood ;" and ſhe may be aſſured, they will continue to do ſo; but, for her comfort, ſhe has the faithful promiſe of him, with whom it is impoſſible to lie; " That the ſpirit of the " Lord ſhall lift up the ſtandard againſt them," Iſa. lix. 19. And therefore, ſhe may adopt the words of the Pſalmiſt, even in troublous times; Pſal. xxxii. 7. " Thou " art my hiding place, thou ſhalt preſerve me from " trouble ; thou ſhalt compaſs me about with ſongs of " deliverance. Selah."

4. The

4. The Church is his dwelling-place, the tabernacle of the moſt High, the houſe wherein he hath choſen to reſt; Pſal. cxxxii. 13. " The Lord hath choſen Zion : He hath " deſired it for his habitation. This is my reſt for ever : " Here will I dwell, for I have deſired it." Jeruſalem is the city of the mighty King, Pſal. xlviii. 2. and therefore he will eſtabliſh her for ever, Pſal. lxxxvii. 5. ſhe is the houſe of his glory, and therefore, the houſe that he will glorify with his preſence.

5. The ſafety, well-fare, and proſperity of the Church, tends to the advancement and manifeſtation of the declarative glory of God in the world ; and therefore he will be her ſafe-guard, and her glory. His wiſdom, power, love, and faithfulneſs, are illuſtriouſly diſplayed in his care of, and conduct about the Church; Pſal. cii. 16. " When " the Lord ſhall build up Zion, he ſhall appear in his " glory."

6. Laſtly, The Church is his own, his treaſure, his peculiar treaſure ; his bride and ſpouſe. True Church-members, are his dear children, the travel of his ſoul, Iſa. liii. 11. Now, every one naturally cares for his own. The loving huſband will not ſee the wife of his boſom ſuffer wrong, while it is in his power to afford her help : Nor the affectionate father the children he dearly loves : And are we once to ſuppoſe, that the Father of mercies, in whom compaſſions flow, will not vindicate and defend thoſe from all real hurt and injury, upon whom he has fixed his everlaſting love ?

V. The fifth thing in the method, was to make ſome improvement of the ſubject. And,

The firſt uſe may be of information.

1. From what has been ſaid, we may ſee, that the Church of God is a ſtrong city, and cannot be removed ; but muſt abide for ever. Her God is her wall of defence, and that round about : And in the midſt of her, he is, and ever will be the glory. " As the mountains are " round about Jeruſalem, ſo the Lord is round about his " people, from hencefurth ever for ever," Pſal. cxxv. 2. With what ſweet delictation, may all the genuine children of Zion ſing that ſong ! Iſa. xxvi. 1. " We have a ſtrong

C

" city;

" city ; falvation will God appoint for walls and bulwarks."
Seeing God hath made Jerufalem's walls falvation, her
citizens fhould make her gates praife.

2. We may fee, whence it is, that the Church is faid
to be beautiful as Tirzah, comely as Jerufalem, and terrible as an army with banners. Why, her God is a wall
of fire round about her, and the glory in the midft of her.
This fufficiently accounts, not only for her beauty, but alfo for the terror and amazement, into which her moft
potent adverfaries have been fometimes caft, upon the very fight of her ; Pfal. xlviii. 4, 5, 6. " For lo, the kings
" were affembled, they paffed by together. They faw
" it, and fo they marvelléd ; they were troubled, and
" hafted away. Fear took hold upon them there, and pain,
" as of a woman in travail."

3. We may fee, that the Church is not only a ftrong city, and terrible to her enemies ; but fhe is likewife a city
compactly built together. She hath her wall round about
her. " Jerufalem is builded as a city that is compact toge-
" ther," Pfal. cxxii. 3. The whole city is joined and compac-
ted together with her wall of fire. All the true citizens,
are, by a real and vital union, joined to him, who is the
glory in the midft of them. And, being-unite unto him,
and confequently to one another in him, they have all communion with him, and with one another in him, fuitable to
the nature of that union. He is round about the city, not
only as a wall of defence, but alfo as a wall of conjunction.
He is the head, Col. ii. 19. " From which all the body,
" by joints and bands, having nourifhment miniftred, and
" knit together, increafeth with the increafe of God."

4. We may fee, that the Church is a very honourable
fociety. She is a fociety, feparated from, and exalted
above the world. She dwells alone, incircled with her
wall of fire ; and is not reckoned among the nations. As
her God is unto her a wall of conjunction, he is likewife
her wall of feparation from the world, lying in wicked-
nefs. And, as it is the indifpenfible duty of her fpiritual
guides, fo to keep up the hedge of her difcipline, as to
the utmoft of their power, they may feparate between
the precious and the vile : That this is fo little the concern

cern of many who go under the character of minifters in our day, is one of the many fins and provocations for which a holy God may juftly vifit us in a way of righteous judgment. Our Lord Jefus, as for other ends and purpofes, has appointed the feals of the New Covenant, to be a badge of diftinction between fuch as vifibly bear his image, and thofe, who by unfoundnefs in the faith, and immorality in practice, vifibly declare themfelves to be Satan's flaves and vaffals: But, alas! how little regard is paid to this defign of their inftitution, by many who count themfelves ftewards of the grace of God?

5. We may fee, that every attempt to raze Zion to the foundation, is not only beyond expreffion wicked, but alfo moft vain and foolifh, and muft, in the iffue, prove abortive. The kings of the earth may fet themfelves, and the rulers may take counfel together, againft the Lord, and againft his anointed: But he who fitteth in heaven, fhall laugh, and he who is the glory in the midft of the Church, fhall hold them in derifion, Pfal. ii. 2, 3, 4. The word is gone out of his mouth, with whom it is impoffible to lie, That no weapon formed againft Zion fhall profper; and that every tongue that fhall rife againft her in judgment, fhe fhall condemn, Ifa. liv. 17.

6. We may fee, that the Church and people of God, have no reafon to envy the men of the world of their glory; what they look upon to be their glory. They confider the riches, honours, profits and pleafures of a vain world, to be their glory. The fons of Laban, called their cattle their glory, Gen. xxxi. 1. But the Church has her God for her glory. The Almighty is her gold; and fhe hath plenty of filver. " I will be the glory in " the midft of her faith the Lord." And to the fame effect is that promife we have, Ifa. lx. 19. " The Lord " fhall be unto thee an everlafting light, and thy God thy " glory." The glory of the Church and people of God fhall continue with them, when all earthly pomp and fplendor, fhall be put under an everlafting vail.

7. We may fee, how much we fhould make it our ftudy and endeavour, to hold faft by a God in Chrift, conftraining him by the prayer of faith to abide with us. His
prefence

prefence with us, is both our fafety and our glory. How careful fhould we be, in our feveral ftations, as minifters and people, not only to receive, but alfo to obferve and keep pure and intire, all fuch religious worfhip and ordinances, **as he** hath appointed in his word ? It is in the way of our teaching ; teaching our people carefully to obferve all things whatfoever he hath appointed and commanded us, (though not for our fo doing) that we can expect him to be round about us as our defence ; as in the midft of us, as our glory.

8. We may fee, how little fuch as would defire to be faithful to Chrift, and feek the good of fpiritual Jerufalem, in a backfliding day, need to regard the reproach and contempt that is poured upon them by an apoftatifing generation. When reproached for lifting up a teftimony for the covenanted principles of the Church of Scotland, and endeavouring in our places and ftations, to profecute the ends thereof, in oppofition to the awful fpeat of apoftafy both in principle and practice, which is prevailing in our day : Let us, inftead of being afhamed on that account, rather join with fuch as have fhared the fame lot before us ; in rejoicing that we are counted worthy to fuffer fhame for his name, Acts v. 41. He is with fuch, as through grace, endeavour to act faithfully for him, and that both as their defence and glory. And wherein is the reproach of the world to be accounted of ?

9. Is the Lord the glory in the midft of the Church ? Then his Church and people fhould glory in him. This is the indifpenfible duty of all the children of Zion, Pfal. cxlix. 2. " Let Ifrael rejoice in him that made him : Let " the children of Zion be joyful in their King." Let them rejoice and be very glad, in what he is, in and to Jerufalem. In what he has done for her already, and in what he is telling us he will ftill continue to do for her ; while he faith, " I will be unto her a wall of fire round " about, and the glory in the midft of her."

10. *Laftly,* We may fee matter of comfort to fuch as are caft down on account of the low ftate of matters in the Church at this day. It is true, indeed, there are many ready to fay, that matters are very comfortable at

prefent, with refpeſt to the Church : Say they, the Church enjoys the countenanĉe of the civil magiſtrate ; we have external peace, and we enjoy freedom of fentiment ; and there are no outward lets or impediments laid in the way of the progrefs and advancement of religion. But however defirable thefe things may be in themfelves, matters are neverthelefs low in the Church in our day. Purity in doƈtrine is greatly on the decline in this land, and has been fo now for a long time paſt : The heritage of the Lord is oppreffed by violent intrufions, whereby the pulpits in Scotland are daily filled with a time-ferving miniſtry, who, in a great meafure, content themfelves with the fleece, without evidencing much regard for the flock. The fword of difcipline is feldom drawn, except it be a-gainſt fuch as offer any mite of teſtimony againſt the prevailing apoſtafy of the age. And a fcheme is of late fet up amongſt us under the fpecious and plaufible pretext of Catholic Love, for uniting Eraſtians, Independents, &c. with Prefbyterians, in miniſterial and chriſtian communion; whereby an unthinking generation is tempted to believe, either, that the glorious Head of the Church has appointed no certain form of government to be obferved therein ; or elfe, that it is not worth the contending for. And though the Lord, in his adorable providence, has, in his kindnefs to the generation, brought a teſtimony to the field, againſt the prefent courfe of backfliding from attained-unto reformation ; it is to be lamented, that faid teſtimony, in place of having the defired effeƈt, is, by the bulk of the generation, either treated as the objeƈt of their rage, fcorn and contempt ; or elfe. in a carelefs and indifferent manner, totally negleƈted ; while few, comparatively confidered, are difpofed to take part with it, and endeavour, through grace, to profecute the ends of it.

But however low matters are with us, and though the night fhould yet be darker ; yet, none who defire to favour the duſt of Zion, need defpair of a reviving time ; but let them look to the promife in the text, and the many like words, the Lord has put upon record for the comfort of the mourners in Zion. And let them remember, he is faithful who hath promifed ; let them plead the promife

mife in faith, and wait for au anfwer in the Lord's own
time ; for he will arife and have mercy upon Zion yet,
and the time to favour her fhall come, the time that he
hath fet. And when he appears in his glory to build up
Zion, he will regard the prayer of the deftitute, and not
defpife their prayer, Pfal. cii. 17.

The *laft* ufe of the doctrine, may be in a few exhorta-
tions. And,

1. Let us who are called to act in the capacity of Minifters of the Gofpel, be exhorted to blefs the Lord for all
the kindnefs he has fhewed to his Church and people here-
tofore ; that he has hitherto been a wall of fire round about
her, and the glory in the midft of her. Let us blefs his holy
name, for all the glorious things, and good and comfortable words he has fpoken concerning Zion, refpecting the
time to come ; and particularly for this promife ; that he
will ever be " a wall of fire round about her, and the
" glory in the midft of her."

Let us be concerned to walk about Zion, and go round
about her, telling her towers, marking her bulwarks, and
and confidering her palaces : That we may tell the children
of Zion for their comfort, and thofe who are yet aliens
to the common-wealth of Ifrael, for their encouragement
to caft in their lot with them : That this God is our God
for ever and ever ; and that he will be our guide even
unto death, Pfal. xlviii. 12, 13, 14.

Let us be exhorted, not to fall under unbelieving difcouragements about the Lord's work in the Church ; however low it is at prefent; or however much lower it may
yet come to be. Tho' there are but few appearing to
embrace a teftimony for the purity of doctrine, the juft and
impartial exercife of difcipline, and for prefbyterial Church-
government, in oppofition to Eraftianifm on the one hand,
and Independency upon the other, with the latitudinarian
tenets, which are propogated amongft us : However this
may afford us matter of lamentation, it is no juft caufe,
why we fhould give way to unbelieving difcouragements.
For it is not by might, nor by power of human kind, that
the Lord ordinarily carries on his work ; but by his fpirit:
And how few, and weakfoever the inftruments are, he is
pleafed

pleafed to make ufe of in his work, they are fufficient in his hand to carry it forward : Let us then ftudy daily to comfort ourfelves, and one another with thefe' words, and that amidft all that is difcouraging. " I, faith the " Lord, will be unto her a wall of fire round about, and " will be the glory in the midft of her."

2. Let me exhort you who are the people of God, the true and genuine children of fpiritual Jerufalem, planted in the houfe of our God, not merely in refpect of external privilege, but by his grace.

Let me exhort you,

1. To blefs the Lord for bringing you (who were by nature aliens to the common-wealth of Ifrael, and ftrangers to the covenant of promife) to be fellow citizens with the faints, and of the houfehold of faith. Great is the reafon you have to blefs the Lord on this account : For now, God is your God, your glory, and the uplifter of your heads. You are in a ftate of fafety, let the worft come to the worft. No real evil can poffibly befal you, nor plague come near your dwelling. God, as your God in covenant, is, and for ever will be, a wall of fire round about you ; and he will alfo be your glory.

2. Give all diligence to walk worthy of the vocation wherewith you are called, ftudying in all things to pleafe God, approving yourfelves unto him in all things; and leaving it for your unfeigned defire to be approven of by him. Let your light fo fhine before thofe among whom you live, in a holy life, and favoury converfation, as that they, beholding your works, may glorify your Father who is in heaven ; and that ftrangers to Chrift may be excited and ftirred up by your example, to come into the fame happy condition with yourfelves.

3. We exhort you, not to be afhamed of our Lord Jefus, of his truths, words, and ways, before a perverfe generation. But, remember, that the clofeft attachment to all his truths, ordinances, and inftitutions, is your honour and crown. Be concerned always to bear in mind, that whatever you may at any time fuffer for cleaving to Chrift with purpofe of heart, you have this for your encouragement under it, That he hath faid to Jerufalem and

all

all her genuine children, That he will be unto them a wall
of fire round about, and the glory in the midst of them.

Lastly, As to you who are only inhabitants of spiritual
Jerusalem in name and profession, but not in reality. We
exhort you to consider, that a name to live among men,
will not avail you in the day of trial, and particularly in
the day of death, if you continue dead in trespasses and
sins. However long you may hide your hypocrisy under
the vail of a plausible profession, yet, remember, the day
is hasting on, when *the sinners in Zion shall be afraid, and
fearfulness will surprise the hypocrite*. Be exhorted, then,
to unite with the Lord Jesus by faith, and you shall henceforth, be in a safe and most honourable and happy condition, having a three-one God in Christ, a wall of fire
round about you, and being possessed of him, as your
everlasting glory. " For I, saith the Lord, will be unto
" her a wall of fire round about, and will be the glory in
" the midst of her."

THE END.

aithfulnefs unto Death in the fervice of
CHRIST, gratuitoufly rewarded with
a Crown of Life.

A

S E R M O N,

Preached at the opening of the ASSOCIATE SYNOD, at
Edinburgh, September 3. 1776.

GAL. vi. 9.

*And let us not be weary in well-doing : For in due feafon we
shall reap, if we faint not.*

E D I N B U R G H:
PRINTED in the Year 1777.

A a b c d e f g h
J K L M N O P q r
ſ S t U V W x y z

A a b c d e f g h i J k l m n o p q r
ſ S t U V W x y z x

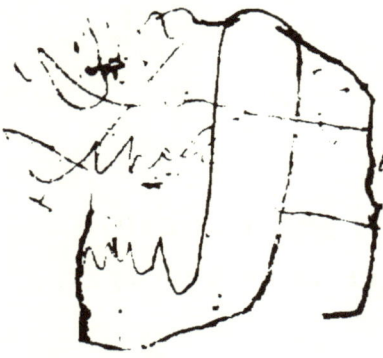

REV. ii. 10. last clause.

Be thou faithful unto death, and I will give thee a crown of
life.

THESE words are a part of that sweet and comfortable epistle, which John, the Disciple whom Jesus
loved, wrote by Divine direction, unto the Angel of the
Church in Smyrna, in Asia the lesser. In which, as the
case of this Church did greatly differ from the condition
of some of the rest to whom he also wrote, and that, both
in respect of suffering and integrity: The message sent
to her, is likewise very dissimilar to those directed to
them. There is no charge exhibited against this Church;
but all that is spoken to her, runs in the amiable stile of
commendation and approbation. Not, that we are once
to suppose, that either ministers or people were altogether
without failings and short-comings in the way of duty;
but they were free from gross heresies and scandals, sincerely aiming at their duty in their places and stations;
and all this, amidst the perplexing disadvantages of po-
verty and persecution: And therefore her kind and sym-
pathizing Head, was graciously pleased to pass over her
infirmities.

In the preface to this Epistle, our Lord Jesus takes
such names and designations to himself, as tended best to
suit the case and circumstances of those to whom it was
directed. These things, saith the first and the last, who
was dead, and is alive. He who was dead, that he might
procure the Crown of Life for you, and is alive again, to
set it upon your heads when once your course is finished.

In the body of the epistle, our Lord declares, that he
was not only most intimately acquainted with the present
condition of this Church, but he likewise informs her,
that her future trials were already present to his all-see-
ing eye. " I know thy works, and tribulations, and po-

D 2   " verty;

" verty ; but thou art rich," rich in faith and good works, though outwardly poor, poor in reality, and poor in the world's efteem. He comforts her under prefent trials, and encourages her in the profpect of future tribulations. *I know thy works*, that is, I approve of thy works : And fuch a declaration was truly comforting for the prefent. And as to what fhe had yet to fuffer, he faith, *Fear none of thefe things* : Which words, taken in their connection, are not merely to be taken as an exhortation to duty, but as alfo containing a promife of all needful comfort and fupport under whatever fufferings were yet before her hand. And in the faith's perfuafion of this being her privilege, fhe is exhorted to perfevere in the way of duty to the end ; knowing, her labour fhould not be in vain in the Lord : " Be thou faithful unto death, " and I will give thee a crown of life." In which words,

1*ft*, We have a moft pathetic exhortation tendered, *Be thou faithful unto death.*

2*dly*, A moft fweet and encouraging motive to enforce the exhortation. *I will give thee a crown of life.*

In the exhortation we may notice,

1. To whom it is directed ; and that is to the angel, miniftry, or office-bearers in the Church of Smyrna, as is obvious from the direction of the epiftle, ver. 8. Yet, the exhortation is not fo to them as to exclude the people under their charge ; being equally bound, in their places and ftations, to the performance of the duty enjoined, with thofe who were over them in the Lord ; and ftanding in as much need of direction, in the way of duty, and encouragement in order to their perfevering therein to the end, as they did.

2. We have the exhortation itfelf, *Be thou faithful.* As if our Lord had faid, ftedfaftly maintain your faith in, faithfulnefs to, and dependence upon me in the feveral ftations wherein I have called you to act.

3. We may obferve the period fet to the duty of faithfulnefs in the fervice of Chrift ; namely, the moment of our departure out of this world. " Be thou faithful " unto death." There may be fome of you, as if our Lord had faid, who may have to refift unto blood in the
way

way of faithfulnefs to me. And, if it fhould be fo, faithfulnefs is ftill your indifpenfible duty ; and what the Spirit
faid to this Church, he is ftill faying to all the churches
of the faints. He is in the fame manner befpeaking every
one of us, Be thou faithful unto death ; faithful unto the
laft, whatever your fo being hath, or may yet coft you.

In the motive to enforce the exhortation, notice,

1. A gracious reward annexed to faithfulnefs. A
crown. I will give thee a crown. This promifed
crown, is expreffive of all that glory and felicity, the faints
are eternally to poffefs in the world to come.

2. We may obferve the nature and quality of this
crown ; and it is, without controverfy, of all crowns the
moft to be defired ; a Crown of life. Eternal glory is
here defigned a crown of life, as oppofed to the prefent
condition of this Church, and to what fome in it were
likely to lofe for Chrift, viz. a natural life. Our Lord
promifes, that though they fhould lay down a temporal
life in his fervice, they fhould moft certainly be crowned with all the felicity and glory of an eternal one.

3. We may obferve how this crown is to be conferred,
and that is in the way of free gift. Our Lord does not
fay, be faithful unto death, and fo merit a crown of life
unto yourfelves. No, but be thou faithful unto death,
and I will moft freely and gratuitoufly give you the
crown. Though this inriching and dignifying crown is
only to be expected in the way of our being faithful in
the fervice of Chrift, yet, it is by no means to be beftow-
ed upon us on the account of our faithfulnefs.

4. We may obferve from whom this crown is to be
expected, and that is our Lord Jefus Chrift. He who is
the firft and the laft ; and who was dead, and is alive
again. He who was gracioufly pleafed to wear the crown
of thorns and the purple robe, that we might wear the
crown of life, and the garments of falvation. He who
once had the burden of purchafing the crown of life, and
now enjoys the honour actually to beftow it upon all the
heirs of promife.

5. Laftly, We may obferve the certainty of the promife ; I, fays Chrift, will give thee a crown of life. I promife

mife it to you, I who am *the Amen, the faithful and true Witnefs*, and fo cannot deceive you. Be thou faithful, and I will not fail to give thee the crown. He may juftly command what he will, who can both promife and alfo perform whatever he pleafes.

From this view of the words, we obferve the following doctrine.

Doct. As our Lord Jefus requires, that all who ferve him, do it faithfully, whatever their doing fo may coft them : So he has, for their encouragement, gracioufly engaged himfelf, by promife, in due time, to crown them with eternal life.

In fpeaking to this doctrine, as the Lord may be pleafed to enable, The method I fhall obferve, is,

I. To fpeak of the duty enjoined, *be thou faithful unto death.*

II. Offer fome thoughts concerning the gracious reward, *the crown of life.*

III. Enquire a little into the connection there is betwixt faithfulnefs unto death in the fervice of Chrift, and the enjoyment of the crown of life.

IV. Make fome improvement of the whole.

The firft thing is, to fpeak of the duty enjoined, " Be " thou faithful unto death." And we fhall, on this occafion, chiefly confider it as refpecting the minifters of Chrift, except in fo far as it may fall under confideration in the improvement of the fubject, as refpecting all who ferve our Lord Jefus, in whatever ftation. The duty of minifterial faithfulnefs then, may be viewed, as refpecting a three-fold object : 1*ft*, Jefus Chrift their great Lord and Mafter. 2*dly*, Themfelves. 3*dly*, The people committed to their charge.

1*ft*, The minifters of Chrift are to be faithful to him : To be fo is their indifpenfible duty, their greateft honour ; and, through grace, it will be their higheft ambition.

tion. Now, for minifters of the gofpel to be faithful to Chrift, will be found to include the following things :

1. Their having his call to act in that high and honourable ftation. None can act faithfully for Chrift, who runs unfent. Our Lord himfelf, took not upon him the honour of the Mediatorial office without his Father's call and appointment ; Heb. v. 4, 5. " And no man taketh " this honour unto himfelf, but he who is called of God, " as was Aaron : So alfo Chrift glorified not himfelf to be " made an High Prieft ; but he who faid unto him, Thou " art my Son, to-day have I begotten thee." Faithful Prophets were fent, and Apoftles and Evangelifts had their commiffion from Chrift ; and though extraordinary gifts and office-bearers, are now ceafed, and an immediate call to the miniftry, no more to be expected : Yet, the Lord ftill continues to call men to the work of the gofpel, in an ordinary and mediate way ; and that by inclining their hearts to ferve him in the gofpel of his Son, furnifhing them with a competent meafure of gifts and prudence ; and opening a door in his providence, by which they may enter into his fervice, in an orderly and regular manner.

2. Faith in Chrift. Faithfulnefs to him, fprings from faith in him. To be faithful to Chrift, is to pleafe God ; but without faith, it is impoffible to pleafe him ; Heb xi. 6. David faith, " I have believed, therefore have I fpoken." And to the fame purpofe fpeaks the Apoftle Paul, 2 Cor. iv. 13. " We having the fame fpirit of faith, according as " it is written, I believed, and therefore have I fpoken : " We alfo believe, and therefore fpeak."

3. Some tolerable meafure of knowledge and acquaintance with the feveral parts of the work and fervice he calls for at their hands. All faithful fervice performed to Chrift, is founded in the knowledge of his will, as manifefted in his word : And all who are in reality his faithful fervants, have not only a fpeculative knowledge of his will as externally revealed ; but alfo fome meafure of faving and internal acquaintance therewith. All who have ever been brought to believe in Chrift, and to act faithfully for him, have heard and learned of the Father ; John vi. 45. They

They have that knowledge of divine things, that flesh and blood cannot give, but our Father who is in heaven.

4. A cordial and hearty acquiescing in, and compliance with their Master's will, so far as they discern and take it up, without consulting with flesh and blood, or setting up self-will, wisdom, or carnal ease, in competition therewith. The Apostle Paul, that most eminently faithful servant of Jesus Christ, tells us, that when it pleased God to reveal his Son in him, that he should preach him among the heathen, he did not confer with flesh and blood, Gal. i. 16.

5. A real and hearty concern for the advancement of his honour and declarative glory, in every part of the work he employs them in where faithfulness to Christ really obtains among the ministers of the gospel. In preaching the word, there will be a single eye to his glory, in the salvation of their souls among whom they labour. They will not preach themselves; seek their own honour, nor hunt after the applause of men; but will, through grace, sincerely endeavour that God in all things may be glorified, 2 Cor. iv. 5. "We preach not ourselves, but " Christ Jesus the Lord; and ourselves your servants for " Jesus sake." In their judicative capacities, they will faithfully endeavour to judge for the Lord, who, in their so doing, is with them in the judgment. They will be conscientiously careful to decide controversies, and apply the censures of the Church without knowing faces, or acting partially: Well knowing, that the soul of the peasant is as precious in the sight of their great Lord, as that of the prince. The spirit of God calls ministers to be faithful in this matter, in the most pressing and solemn manner, 1 Tim. v. 20, 21. "Them who sin rebuke be- " fore all, that others also may fear. I charge thee be- " fore God and the Lord Jesus Christ, and the elect An- " gels, that thou observe these things, without prefer- " ring one before another, doing nothing by partiality."

In so far as they are instrumental in putting men into the ministry, they will be careful to commit the word of reconciliation into the hands of faithful men; at least faithful as they suppose; 2 Tim. ii. 2. "And the things " which thou hast heard of me among many witnesses, the
" same

fame commit thou to faithful men, " who fhall be able
" to teach others alfo ;" and to the fame purpofe is
that we have, 1 Tim. v. 22. " Lay hands fuddenly on
" no man, neither be partaker of other mens fins ; keep
" thyfelf pure." It is moft finful for thofe who are
naughty to prefs themfelves into the miniftry ; and in fo
far as any are inftrumental in giving encouragement to
fuch, they are partakers with them in their fin.

6. Faithfulnefs to Chrift has in it an earneft and hearty
concern for the maintenance of the truth, and the prefervation of the purity of all his ordinances. Faithful minifters are fet for the defence of the gofpel of Chrift, and
difpofed through grace, to keep by the word of his patience, Rev. iii. 10. Which may be underftood of any of the
truths of Chrift, which comes more immediately to be con-
troverted and oppofed by men of corrupt minds.

7. *Laftly,* To be faithful unto Chrift in the work of
the miniftry, has in it, not only a real defire to ferve
their own generation, according to the will of God, but
alfo, the ufing of their beft endeavours to hand down a
teftimony for the purity of gofpel doctrine, difcipline and
worfhip to the generations yet to come. As alfo, for that
form of government the Lord Jefus has appointed to be
obferved in the church ; which form of government is
neither Eraftian on the one hand, nor Independent on the
other ; but Prefbyterial. Confifting in the due fubordina-
tion of one judicatory to another. As is clear from
Math. xviii. 15,—19. chap. xvi. 19. Acts xiii. 1,—4.
1 Tim. iv. 14. Acts xv. with many other texts which
might be adduced. That Prefbytery is the only form of
government the Lord Jefus has appointed to be obferved in the Church, is made evident to every unprejudifed
mind, in the propofitions concerning Church-government,
bound in with our excellent Confeffion of Faith ; together
with feveral other learned tracts, which have been wrote
on that fubject by divines, eminent both for learning and
piety ; and thefe not only in this, but alfo in our neigh-
bouring kingdoms, in their contending for Prefbytery
againft Eraftians on the one fide, and thofe of the Independent perfuafion on the other. A teftimony for thefe

E things,

things, fuch as would defire mercy of the Lord to be
faithful, will be concerned to tranfmit to pofterity. This
we are, by the Spirit of God, moft earneftly called to do,
Pfal. lxxviii. 5, 6, 7. " He eftablifhed a teftimony in Ja-
" cob, and appointed a law in Ifrael, which he command-
" ed our fathers, that they fhould make them known to
" their children : That the generation to come might
" know them, even the children which fhould be born ;
" who fhould arife and declare them to their children :
" That they might fet their hope in God, and not forget
" the works of God, but keep his commandments." The
fame duty is enjoined us, Pfal. xlviii. 12, 13, 14.
" Walk about Zion, and go round about her : Tell the
" towers thereof. Mark ye well her bulwarks, confider
" her palaces ; that ye may tell it to the generations fol-
" lowing. For this God is our God for ever and ever ;
" he will be our guide even unto death."

2dly, Minifters of the gofpel are to be faithful to themfelves ; and if they would be fo indeed, they will find it
abfolutely needful to be unite to the perfon of Chrift by
faith, as their Saviour and Redeemer : That their hearts
be right with God, and found in his ftatutes. They will
find themfelves under an indifpenfible neceffity to make a
home and particular application of the truths they deliver
unto others, to their own fouls. If they would be found
faithful to themfelves, they will endeavour in the ftrength
of grace, to put the duties in practice themfelves which
they recommend to their hearers. While they keep the
vineyard of the church, they will carefully watch over
their own. They will not fail to endeavour to fet the
duties of religion before their people, not only in the pulpit, but alfo by a tender and circumfpect walk and converfation. If thefe and fuch like things are not to be
found in the character of the gofpel minifters, after they
have preached Chrift to others, they may themfelves be
caft-away, and in the end be led furth with the workers
of iniquity, 1 Cor. ix. 26, 27. " I therefore fo run, not
" as uncertainly ; fo fight I, not as one that beateth the
" air : But I keep under my body, and bring it into fub-
" jection : Left that by any means, when I have preached
" to others, I myfelf fhould be a caft-away."

3dly, Minifterial

3*dly*, Ministerial faithfulness has a respect to those of whose souls ministers of the gospel under Christ have the charge. And for ministers to be faithful to those they are over in the Lord, carries in it:

1. Their preaching sound doctrine, free from and unmixed with the leaven of error and heresy. Concerning this, the apostle Paul gives Titus a charge, and in him all the ministers of Christ to the end of time, chap. ii. 1. " But speak thou the things which become sound doc- " trine." And he adds, ver. 7, 8.. " In doctrine shewing " uncorruptness, sound speech that cannot be condemned." And Timothy is exhorted to hold fast the form of sound words, 2 Tim. i. 13. These and the many like directions tendered in the word of God, ministers of the gospel must carefully attend unto, as they would be found faithful to those committed to their charge; and for that end, should be much in the study of the scriptures, joined with fervent prayer, that the Spirit of God may guide them into all the truth, according to our Lord's most gracious promise, John xvi. 12, 13. They should moreover, give themselves to the reading of approven systems of divinity, among which our excellent standards justly claim the precedency, and, comparing scripture with scripture, they ought to give the most heedful attention to the analogy of faith.

2. A real endeavour, according to their capacity and measure of knowledge, to keep back nothing from their hearers, that they judge, as in the sight of God, may tend to the edification of their souls. This is what the apostle Paul calls the *not shunning to declare the whole counsel of God*, Acts xx. 27. And while nothing is to be kept back, faithful ministers will not fail to insist most upon these truths which are of greatest moment and weight. Such as the depravity of man's nature, his misery of consequence, with his utter inability to do any thing for his own recovery out of the snare of the devil. The way of his recovery by virtue of the undertaking, incarnation, life, death, resurrection and intercession of the Son of God. The truths respecting the person of Christ, his fulness of saving offices, and justifying and sanctifying grace. With
the

the way in which finful men come really to have an intereft in him, with all his riches of grace and glory; which is only by union to his perfon, through the faith of his fpirit's opperation; Eph. ii. 8. " By grace are ye faved, " through faith ; and that not of yourfelves: It is the " gift of God."

3. Minifters who would be found faithful to thofe under their charge, will find it highly needful to take heed, how, as well as what they preach.

They will find caufe to do it plainly, in imitation of him whofe alone province it is to declare the whole counfel of God. He preached moft plainly. When he was pleafed to ufe fimilitudes, tho' he could have fetched them from the heights above, or from the deeps beneath; yet, he was pleafed to take them from thefe objects and cuftoms with which his hearers were moft intimately acquaint. Yea, fo very condefcending was he in his manner of teaching, that he fometimes fpeaks as if he had been at a lofs to know how he might beft adapt his difcourfe to the capacities of his hearers ; Mark xiv. 30. " Where- " unto (faith he,) fhall we liken the kingdom of God, or " with what comparifon fhall we compare it ?"

They will find it highly expedient, to fet the truths of the gofpel before their people, in a clear, diftinct, concife and connected manner; fo as that the connection with, and dependence of one truth upon another, may readily appear to their underftandings. Thofe truths they bring forth unto their hearers, they are to feek out, and fet in order before hand, after the example of the Royal Preacher in Ifrael, Eccl. xii. 9. Such as defire to be faithful to the fouls of thofe for whom they watch, will not put them off with that which coft them nothing.

Faithfulnefs, as to the manner of preaching the gofpel, carries in it, the delivering of the truth with fuch a meafure of boldnefs, gravity and earneftnefs, as may give the hearers to know, they are really in earneft to have their meffage received. Thus dealt the apoftle Paul with thofe to whom he preached and wrote, Rom. xii. 1. " I be- " feech you," fays he to the Romans, " Brethren, by " the

" the mercies of God, that ye prefent your bodies a liv-
" ing facrifice, holy, acceptable unto God, which is your
" reafonable fervice." Moreover, they muft lay before
their hearers, the greatnefs of their fin, with the danger
they will expofe themfelves unto, if they receive not the
truth in the love of it, that they may be faved. They
muft be given to know, that fuch as believe not, fhall be
damned, Mark xvi. 16. And that final neglectors of the
falvation exhibited in the gofpel, can by no means efcape
the punifhment of everlafting deftruction from the prefence
of the Lord, when he fhall come to be glorified in his
faints, and admired in all thofe who do believe. -

4. For minifters to be faithful to thofe under their
charge, includes their exciting and ftirring them up carefully to maintain good works, Tit. iii. 8. " This is a
" faithful faying, and thefe things I will that thou affirm
" conftantly, that they who have believed in God, might
" be careful to maintain good works : Thefe things are good
" and profitable unto men." And while they thus call
them to performance of the duties of religion, they will
not fail at the fame time, to lay before them the true
fprings of gofpel holinefs. Namely, deliverance from the
law as a covenant of works, faith's union to the perfon of
Chrift, with conftant dependence upon the Spirit of God
in his grace and gracious influences, for affiftance in order
to the acceptable performance of every duty. Thefe
things we find our Lord infifted much upon to his difciples, John xv. 4. " Abide in me, and I in you. As
" the branch can not bear fruit of itfelf, except it abide
" in the vine : No more can ye, except ye abide in me."
And verfe 8. he adds, " without me ye can do nothing."

And while they muft give men to know, that their
ftrength for the performance of duty is only in Chrift ; they
are, with all poffible care, to guard them againft trufting
to their duties, and religious performances, as being a
foundation upon which they are either in whole, or in
the fmalleft degree, to build their hope of eternal life.
" For by the works of the law fhall no flefh be juftified,"
Gal. ii. 16. and, adds the fame Apoftle, v. 21. " I do
" not fruftrate the grace of God : For if righteoufnefs
" come

" come by the law, then Chrift is dead in vain." Tho' the
end everlafting life, and the means leading thereunto,
muft not, and will not be put affunder by fuch as would
enjoy the crown of life. Yet, it is not to be expected by any, becaufe they ufe thefe means, but only in the
way of the believing improvement of them.

5. If minifters would be faithful to the flocks committed to their charge, they muft be willing to fpend, and
be fpent for their fouls good and edification, and that tho'
it fhould fome times fo fall out, that the more they evidence their love to them in the faithful difcharge of their
duty, the lefs they be beloved of them. They muft
endeavour to ftrengthen the weak, comfort the down-
caft, fympathife with the tempted, warn the unrully, re-
book, reprove and exhort, with all long fuffering and
doctrine. All this is contained in what the Apoftle Paul
tells us he aimed at in all his adminiftrations, Col. i. 28,
29. " We preach, warning every man, and teaching
" every man in all wifdom; that we may prefent every
" man perfect in Chrift Jefus : Whereunto I alfo labour
" ftriving according to his working, which worketh in me
" mightily."

We fhall only further add upon this head, that this
duty of faithfulnefs, as it refpects the above threefold object; is to be perfifted in unto the end. Be thou faithful unto death, and I will give thee a crown of life.
Men are not crowned, except they ftrive lawfully. Ap-
parent faithfulnefs for a while, will not be found a proper
compliance with this exhortation, Gal. iii. 4. Minifters
who would be found faithful, muft count nothing dear,
no not life itfelf, if fo be they would finifh their courfe
with joy, and the miniftry committed unto them, Acts xx.
24. All the oppofition they may meet with in the way of
duty, and all the fcandal that may be caft upon the ways
of God by a profane world on the one hand, or by the
backfliding and apoftafy of profeffed friends upon the other,
muft not prevail with them to take their hand from the
plough : But they muft remember the words of the Lord
Jefus ; " Be thou faithful unto death, and I will give
" thee a crown of life."

II. The

II. The *second* head was to offer some thoughts concerning the gracious reward, promised by Christ to all who serve him faithfully in whatever station he is pleased in his providence to put them ; and it is here called a crown of life. And as we are hereby to understand all that honour, felicity and glory, of which the saints are to be possessed in the heavenly rest.

First, We may consider the glory in reserve for the saints, as a crown.

Secondly, As a crown of life.

It was first proposed to consider the glory in reserve for the saints as a crown. Wherefore is the glory to be revealed, called a crown ?

1. It is so called, to point forth the exceeding greatness of that honour and dignity to be conferred upon the people of God in the heavenly rest. A crown is an emblem of majesty, and denotes the kingly and imperial dignity, wherewith they are to be invested. They are the children of the king, the King of kings. Yea, they are themselves kings and priests unto God, Rev. i. 6. They are in their regeneration, born heirs unto a kingdom that cannot be moved, and which it is their Father's good pleasure to give them, Luke xii. 32. And they must have a crown ; and for a throne, the Captain of Salvation will give them to sit with him in his throne, Rev. iii. 21. " To him that overcometh, will I give to sit with me in " my throne, even as I also overcame, and am set " down with my Father in his throne."

2. Glory is called a crown, to set forth the fulness and perfection of the felicity of the saints. A crown is of that figure and make, that it incircles the whole head; and the saints will be possessed of glory, both objectively, in their being admitted into the immediate vision and fruition of God, and subjectively, in their likeness and conformity to him. Hence saith the Apostle John in his first epistle, chap. iii. 2. " Beloved, now are we the sons of God, " and it doth not yet appear what we shall be ; but we " know, that when he shall appear, we shall be like him: " For we shall see him as he is." And to the same purpose is that we have, Psal. xvii. 15. " I will behold
" thy

" thy face in righteousnefs. I fhall be fatisfied, when I
" awake, with thy likenefs."

3. Glory is called a crown, to point furth the period
at which the faints are to be admitted to the full enjoyment thereof; and that is not until they fhall be made
compleatly conquerors over all their fpiritual enemies,
through him who loved them. Our Lord feems here to
allude to fome of the cuftoms of running or wreftling,
which obtained much in the eaftern countries, where
thofe who proved victorious, were crowned with fome
garland or crown, as an emblem of victory and conqueft,
I Cor. ix. 24, 25. " Know ye not, (faith the Apoftle,)
" that they who run in a race, run all, but one receiveth
" the prize; fo run that ye may obtain. And every man
" who ftriveth for the maftery, is temperate in all things:
" Now, they do it to obtain a corruptible crown, but
" we an incorruptible."

Secondly, It was propofed upon this head, to confider
the glory to be conferred upon the faints as a crown of
life. It is called a crown of righteoufnefs, 2 Tim. iv. 8.
Henceforth, fays the great Apoftle of the Gentiles, " There
" is laid up for me a crown of righteoufnefs, which the
" Lord the righteous judge fhall give me at that day:"
And left any fhould be ready to think this crown is in re-
ferve only for prophets, apoftles and other faithful minifters, he adds, " And not to me only, but to all them al-
" fo who love his appearing."

It is called a crown of glory, 1 Pet. v. 4. where, after
exhorting gofpel minifters to faithfulnefs and diligence as
an encouragement thereto, he adds, " And when the
" chief Shepherd fhall appear, ye fhall receive a crown of
" glory that fadeth not away."

In James i. 12. it is defigned, as in the text, a crown
of life. " Bleffed is the man who endureth temptation:
" For when he is tried, he fhall recieve the crown of life,
" which the Lord hath promifed to them who love him."
Now,

1. Glory may be called a crown of life, to put us in
mind of what we loft by our fall and apoftafy in the firft
Adam. By our breach of covenant in him, we forfeited
our

our temporal life to the juſtice of God, we loſt a life of fellowſhip with God on earth ; and gave up with all title and claim to eternal life in heaven. Life, eternal life, is the great bleſſing men have loſt by the breach of the firſt covenant; and it is the great and leading bleſſing procured for them by the fulfilment of the ſecond ; Tit. i. 2. " In " hope of eternal life, which God who cannot lie, pro- " miſed before the world began :" And, ſaith the Apoſtle, Rom. vi. 23. " The gift of God is eternal life, through " Jeſus Chriſt our Lord."

2. Glory may be called a crown of life, to ſet furth the myſterious nature thereof. Life has in it ſomething which is full of myſtery. And the Apoſtle tells us, " Eye " hath not ſeen, nor ear heard, neither have entered in- " to the heart of man, the things which God hath pre- " pared for them who love him," 1 Cor. ii. 9. And the ſame Apoſtle, when ſpeaking elſewhere of the glory to be revealed, 2 Cor. iv. 17, 18. He calls it a weight ; a great weight; an exceeding great weight ; and an eter- nal weight of glory. All which expreſſions, do, in the moſt ample manner, ſet before us the inconceivable and myſterious nature of the heavenly inheritance.

3. It may be called life, becauſe life is of all things the moſt ſweet and deſirable. Satan, for once ſpoke the truth, tho' of bad deſign, when he ſaid, " All that a man hath " will he give for his life," Job ii. 4. And if a temporal life, imbittered with ſo many trials, as are become una- voidable by reaſon of ſin, be ſo very deſirable, what muſt an eternal one, crowned with all poſſible felicity, really prove to be?

4. Glory may be called life, to ſet forth the activity of the ſaints in glory. Where there is life, there is ac- tion. Heaven will not only be found to be a place of re- treat from toil, labour and ſorrow ; but alſo a place of moſt active ſervice. There the inhabitants reſt not day nor night, nor yet ſay they are weary, Rev. iv. 8. What their employment is, either as to matter or manner, the day will beſt declare : Only we are ſure, the high praiſes of redeeming love, will forever fill the hearts and mouths of the ranſomed of the Lord ; Iſa. xxxv. 10. " And the

F   " ranſomed

" ranfomed of the Lord fhall return, and come to Zion
" with fongs, and everlafting joy upon their heads: They
" fhall obtain joy and gladnefs, and forrow and fighing
" fhall flee away." And to this agree the words of the
Apoftle ; Rev. v. 9. " And they fung a new fong, fay-
" ing, Thou art worthy to take the book, and to open
" the feals thereof : For thou waft flain, and has re-
" deemed us to God by thy blood, out of every kindred,
" and tongue, and people, and nation."

5. Glory is here called a crown of life as oppofed to
what fome in this Church were likely to lofe for Chrift.
They had fuch an intimation, as that fome of them at
leaft, might lay their account with fuffering marterdom in
their Mafter's caufe. And it is very ordinary in fcripture,
to meet with the heavenly glory fet furth by fuch expreffions as tend to oppofe it to the various calamities the
people of God are moft frequently trifled with in a prefent
world ; fuch as treafure for the poor, reft for the weary,
and joy for the mourner. So here our Lord faith, be
not afraid to lay down a temporal life, if I fhall call for
it ; for when you have fo done, you fhall take up an
eternal one, attended with the moft confummate joy and
felicity.

6. *Laftly,* Glory is called *a crown of life,* to fet furth
the durable and lafting nature thereof. Heaven is an un-
defiled inheritance, and therefore, it fadeth not away.
This crown fhall not wither, nor will the head decay from
under it ; but to eternity it fhall flourifh, when temporal
kingdoms and crowns, pomp and fplendor fhall be no
more. For there the Lord commands the blefling, even
life for evermore.

III. The *third* thing in the method was, to touch a
little at the connection betwixt faithfulnefs to the death
in the fervice of Chrift, and the enjoyment of the crown
of life. And,

1. Let it be obferved, that there is no cafual or me-
ritorious connection. No, to affirm there is, would be to
fly in the face of the leading and chief defign of God in
the whole economy of redemption, which is to fhew the
exceeding

exceeding riches of his grace, in his kindness to us through
Christ Jesus. Free and rich grace shines furth in the con-
trivance of redemption, Job xxxiii. 24. in the purchase
of it, 2 Cor. viii. 9. And it is no less conspicuous and
manifest in the application thereof, Eph. ii. 8. And the
glory to be revealed, is called *grace*, 1 Pet. i. 13. And
the *mercy* of our Lord Jesus Christ, Jude ver. 21.

2. There is nevertheless a connection betwixt faithfulness to the death, and the crown. And that,

1. In the purpose of God, those of whom he has been
pleased to make choice to life everlasting, to them he pur-
posed to give grace in time; and perseverance in it to the
end; and then to crown grace with glory; Rom. viii. 30.
" Moreover, whom he did predestinate, them he also
" called: And whom he called, them he also justified:
" And whom he justified, them he also glorified."

2. In the promise of God, " Be thou faithful unto
" death, and I will give thee a crown of life." A gracious God, tho' he cannot make himself our debtor, has
nevertheless been pleased to make himself debtor to his
own faithfulness pledged in the promise. Hence saith the
Apostle, " God is not unrighteous," that is, he is not
unfaithful " to forget your work and labour of love,
" which ye have shewed toward his name, in that ye have
" ministered to the saints, and do minister," Heb. vi. 10.
The crown then is to be expected in the way of being
faithful; but not on the account of our faithfulness, but
on account of the free and faithful promise of God con-
firmed with the precious blood of Jesus.

3. *Lastly*, There is a connection betwixt faithfulness
and the enjoyment of the crown of life, in respect of evidence. When any are brought by grace to act faithfully
for Christ, and enabled to hold out faithfully to the end;
it is a comfortable evidence to themselves, that theirs is
the kingdom of God. It has also a tendency in some
measure, to evidence it to others; Rev. xxii. 14. " Blef-
" fed are they who do his commandments, that they may
" have a right to the tree of life, and may enter in
" through the gates unto the city." As if our Lord had
said, blessed are they who keep the commandments of
God, and by their so doing, having evidenced themselves

to

to be my real difciples and faithful fervants; fhall have authority and dignity vouchfafed to them by my free grant, to enter upon the full poffeffion of all the bleffed fruits which fpring from me the tree of life. But it is now time we make fome improvement of the fubject, which was the laft thing propofed in the method. And,

The *firft* ufe of the doctrine may be of information :

1. Then, Is a call from Chrift to the work of the miniftry neceffary in order to faithfulnefs to him in that work? Then we may fee what to think of fuch as rufh into the minifterial function, without any proper call thereto. There are many in our day, who affume the character of minifters unto themfelves, without any call whatfoever, except it be fome enthufiaftical impulfe within themfelves. And befides thefe, there are many who climb up into the pulpit by the way of a prefentation, from one who, perhaps, is no friend either to Church or State; and inftead of waiting the call of thofe among whom they propofe to labour, How many intrude themfelves, or are intruded upon the heritage of God, over the belly of all the oppofition they have it in their power to make? And with many of them, the event in the cafe of the flock is, as our Lord tells us it would prove, John x. 5. "A ftranger " will they not follow, but will flee from him : For they " know not the voice of ftrangers." Such as run unfent, and they who hear them, would need ferioufly to confider what the Spirit of God affirms concerning both, Jer. xxiii. 21. 32. " I have not fent thefe Prophets, yet they ran : " I have not fpoken to them, yet they prophefied.—Yet I " fent them not, nor commanded them ; therefore they " fhall not profit this people at all, faith the Lord." From the above texts, and many others which might be mentioned; it is evident, that whatever the Lord may do in fovereignty by the miniftry of fuch as have not his call; they who hear them, have no fcriptural ground upon which they can expect to be profited by them : Nor can they with confidence, pray for a bleffing upon their administrations.

2. We may fee that minifters who are carelefs about the condition of their own fouls, can never be faithful to

our

our Lord Jesus Christ. Tho' such may have gifts,—and not be altogether without success; yet, they cannot be faithful, nor have the eye single for the glory of God in the duties they perform; however good those may be as to the matter of them. How can they, who are untender of their own souls, be really concerned for the welfare of the souls of others? How can such as neglect the worship of God in their families, at least in the morning, recommend it to their hearers to offer unto God the morning and evening sacrifice? How can those, who can with freedom go into, and join with the company of promiscuous dancers, recommend sobriety, chastity and gravity to their hearers? And yet many such there are at this day, who call themselves the ministers of Jesus.

3. We may see what to think of such ministers as are not concerned, to the utmost of their power, to make known the whole mystery of the gospel, the whole counsel of God to their hearers; but keep upon general topics of discourse, without entering into cases of conscience, or applying their doctrine against the prevailing errors and sinful practices of the times; and all this partly owing to a careless disposition, or fear of offending the gay and fashionable part of their audience. While such lay out themselves thus to please men, other than to their edification; they need to consider, that in so far as this prevails with them, they are serving men, and not our Lord Jesus, Gal. i. 10. " If I yet pleased men, I should not " be the servant of Christ."

4. We may see how culpable those ministers are, who do not make it their study and endeavour, to lay the truths of the gospel plainly before their hearers; but either through inattention, or a worse principle; wrap up the truths of the gospel in obscure and ambiguous phrases, and modes of expression, by which means, many who hear them cannot be profited. This, with an affected niceness in the manner of delivery, is what the Apostle Paul calls preaching with the enticing words of man's wisdom, 1 Cor. ii. 4. But what have the wisdom of words, and the enticing words of man's wisdom to do in the matter of preaching a crucified Christ? Seeing, there is no design

of

of God more obvious in the whole œconomy of redemption, than to confound carnal wifdom. I fhall only obferve
here, that tho' an affected way of preaching the gofpel,
and the pains taken by fome, to embellifh it with the
flowers of human rhetoric, may pleafe fome and offend
others, it can profit none ; being fuch a manner of
preaching Chrift, as is exprefsly difallowed by the Holy
Ghoft.

5. Does it belong to the character of faithful minifters
of Chrift, to bear teftimony to all his truths, ordinances
and inftitutions, and efpecially to fuch of them as are
either oppofed or flighted in their day ? Then we may
fee what to think of fome who have of late got up amongft
us, who, tho' they profefs to oppofe themfelves to fome
of the finful meafures carried on by the judicatories of
our national Church, yet, quite overlook any particular
teftimony for the purity of doctrines, and are fo far from
bearing any teftimony for that form of government the
Lord Jefus appointed to be obferved in the Church, that
they, are not afhamed to hold themfelves forth to the
world, as ready to hold minifterial and chriftian communion with Epifcopalians, Independents, or any elfe, whom
their charity may incline them to judge belong to the
houfehold of faith, as occafion may ferve, whatever
their principles be. Is this faithfully to ferve our Lord
Jefus ? Or yet to evidence that much boafted of charity
and Catholic love, either to the prefent or rifing generation ? Or is it not to fay, either Chrift has not appointed
any certain form of Church-government ; or if he has, is
it not to fay, it is not worth the contending for, or taking
any particular notice of ? But thofe men may be ready to
fay, are their not among the various denominations of
Chriftians, fuch as have communion with the Head ?
And if fo, we cannot refufe to receive them in
Church-communion alfo. We fhall only obferve as to
this, we are far from denying but there are among Epifcopalians and Independents, fuch as really belong to the
houfehold of faith : And we as readily grant, that there
is an invifible union to, and communion with Chrift, which
are the privileges of all true believers ; and in virtue of
which,

which, they are all unite to, and have communion with one another in him. But this communion being altogether invisible, such as the union is, it is very different from that open and visible communion men have together in the sacrament of the supper; which is not so directly founded in real vital union to Christ (which is the privilege of true believers only,) as in a professed union to him, and to one another in the truth; being professedly agreed in and about the same principles: So that it is not only warrantable, but in a variety of cases necessary, to refuse to hold sacramental communion, even with such as we may judge in charity do really belong to the Head. And so much the more we are persuaded this is the case with them, so much the more are we bound in duty to testify against what is amiss, either in their principles or practice, Gal. ii. 11. 12. and to withdraw from brethren walking diforderly, whether in respect of principle or practice, is far from being inconsistent with due respect to their persons, or that charity the word of God calls us to have for them; which is, to wish them as well in soul, body, and estate as ourselves, and to be in readiness as occasion serves, to act toward them in a loving and beneficent manner.

It may here further be observed, that while those men have given themselves out to the world, as if they meant in some sort, to oppose the progress of defection in our mother church; they have at the same time, adopted such terms of ministerial and christian communion as she would yet be ashamed of. For tho' it may be perhaps alledged, she refuses few, if any, into her communion who apply for admission; yet, she has not as yet gone all the length, in any judicative capacity, to invite Episcopalians and Independents to communion with her, in her sealing-ordinances.

6. We may see the need ministers of the gospel have to exercise a needy dependence upon the Lord Jesus Christ, and in the prayer of faith, to be much at the throne of his grace, as ever they would be found faithful. Their work is great, and who is sufficient for it? How great a matter is it for them to be faithful? Faithful to Christ, to themselves, and to the souls of those committed to their charge?

7. *Lastly,*

5. *Laſtly*, We may ſee, that tho' the glory of God, is that which we are firſt and principally to have in our eye, in the whole of our conduct; yet, the proſpect of the crown of life, is to be improven in a believing manner, as a ſweet and powerful motive to excite us to the duty of faithfulneſs in our ſeveral ſtations. The lively hope of ſalvation, is an able helmet to the head in the day of trial. " Be thou faithful unto death, and I will " give thee a crown of life."

The *ſecond* uſe may be of exhortation. And,

Firſt, Let us, who are in the ſtation of miniſters of the goſpel, ſuffer the word of exhortation. Be thou faithful unto death ; and in order hereunto,

Let us, being ſenſible of our own inſufficiency for the faithful diſcharge of our duty to Chriſt, ourſelves, the Church in general, or the particular flocks we ſtand more immediately connected with. I ſay, let us be concerned to maintain faith's dependence upon our Lord Jeſus Chriſt, for all that furniture and through-bearing we need in his work. Whatever we need is in him, and we have his moſt gracious promiſe to rely upon, that it ſhall be communicate according to our neceſſities, John. xiv. 13. " Whatſoever ye ſhall aſk the Father in my name, " that will I do, that the Father may be glorified in the " Son."

Let us ſtudy to be more and more acquainted with the duties incumbent upon us in the difficult ſphere in which we are called to move, and for this end, let us be much in the ſtudy of the word of God, joined with fervent prayer.

Let us make Chriſt crucified, the Alpha and Omega of our preaching. Let it be our real and hearty concern, to ſet him before our hearers, as that good all the promiſes contain, as the fulfilment of all the propheſies, and as the ſubſtance of all the types. Let us not be negligent in ſhewing unto men, their abſolute need of an intereſt in him, their hearty welcome to receive him with all his fulneſs, as the free gift of God to them. Let us alſo ſhew them the way in which they can only come to be really and ſavingly intereſted in him, namely, their being brought

by

www.ingramcontent.com/pod-product-compliance
Lightning Source LLC
Chambersburg PA
CBHW032121080426
42733CB00008B/1005